LOVE YOU LIKE CRAZY

KATIE TURNER
AUSTIN MARDON
CATHERINE MARDON

Dedication

For anyone who has ever felt unlovable, let this be a reminder, you are capable and worthy of being loved.

Copyright © 2021 by Austin Mardon
All rights reserved. This book or any portion thereof may not be reproduced or used in any manner whatsoever without the express written permission of the publisher except for the use of brief quotations in a book review or scholarly journal.
First Printing: 2021

Typeset and Cover Design by Kim Huynh

ISBN 978-1-77369-600-3
Golden Meteorite Press
103 11919 82 St NW
Edmonton, AB T5B 2W3
www.goldenmeteoritepress.com

Table of Contents

Preface 1

Chapter 1: Searching for Acceptance 5

Chapter 2: Meeting & Disclosing 10

Chapter 3: Dating & Discrimination 15

Chapter 4: I Do 20

Chapter 5: Making Adjustments 25

Chapter 6: Marriage and Mental Illness 30

Chapter 7: Supporting Each Other 34

Chapter 8: Foster Kids 39

Chapter 9: Couples Counselling 44

Chapter 10: Working Together 48

Chapter 11: I Still Love You Like Crazy 51

References 56

Preface

Receiving a psychological diagnosis can feel like your life has been flipped upside down. You might worry about how you can hide it or what people will think when they find out. It can feel like no one will accept you or love you and it can be extremely isolating. In actuality, mental health conditions are quite common. Most research says one in five people will experience a mental health challenge in their lifetime. That number is likely low because it doesn't account for people who don't seek help. About 38% of the Canadian population is married and this doesn't include the people who are in relationships but unmarried (Statistics Canada, 2020). Looking at those two statistics together, it's likely many people will either have a mental health condition or be in a relationship with someone who does. However, there continues to be a lot of stigma surrounding mental illness and relationships. Often they're two things we don't think of together.

People who have a mental illness are increasingly being portrayed in the media, but repeatedly they've been misrepresented which perpetuates misinformation and stigma. Characters who have a mental illness are particularly popular in the horror genre or as villains in other genres. More often than not, they're depicted as especially violent or dangerous. For example, in the movies American Psycho, Split, and Joker, the main characters have a mental illness which plays a large role in them becoming murderers. The stereotype that all people who have a mental illness are violent causes fear and misunderstanding which is harmful. While mental illness has been portrayed in horror, action, and drama films, representation is seriously lacking in the romance genre. Few romance movies or tv shows have a character who has a mental illness and even fewer have said character as the main love interest. If they do happen to be the main love interest, mental illness tends to be romanticized, making it seem glamorous rather than accurately depicting what it's really like to live with a mental illness. Sometimes the character's mental illness and all of their challenges disappear when they fall in love which isn't accurate. Misinterpretations and lack of representation in the media is damaging for people who live with a mental illness. We hope this book can be an accurate representation of having a mental illness and how having mental health challenges doesn't mean you can't have a healthy and long lasting relationship.

Austin and Catherine Mardon both have experience living with a mental illness. They also have been married for over fifteen years, have been foster parents, and run a non-profit agency together. Although this book will focus on how their mental illnesses have impacted their lives and relationship, it's important to remember it's just a small aspect of their lives. Austin is an author, adjunct professor at the University of Alberta, member of the Order of Canada, mentor, brother, and husband. Catherine is an author, lawyer, baritone player, sister, mentor, and wife. Although this is nowhere near an exhaustive list of their accomplishments and roles, it's a reminder they are so much more than a diagnosis.

'Crazy' has often been used as a derogatory way to describe someone who has a mental illness. However, some people are beginning to reclaim the term by using it according to their own definition. Austin often calls himself crazy but in the context that he's taking on projects other people wouldn't even consider trying. This summer he agreed to mentor 360 students, a feat other professors he spoke to said they wouldn't dare consider. The Mardons call themselves crazy for fostering young men who have mental illnesses because other people can't seem to understand why they do it. Love You Like Crazy is another way for the Mardons to reclaim the word. Crazy is used in the sense that they love each other beyond logic or reason and it's not always understood by other people. People call Austin crazy because he has schizophrenia and they call Catherine even crazier for marrying him. In these instances the use of the word crazy is derogatory and unkind. It implies there's something wrong with Austin because of his mental illness, which is untrue and harmful. Although Austin and Catherine use the term crazy for themselves, it's a personal choice. Not everyone with a mental illness shares the same perspective and it's important to be respectful and know when using the term is okay and not okay. Using crazy to negatively describe anyone is harmful especially in clinical settings or towards people who have a mental illness (Gold, 2019). Language can be destructive and stigmatizing which is why it's essential to educate yourself on it.

It's also important to remember this book is based specifically on the Mardons' experiences. Other people who have mental health conditions may have a completely different experience. Even if two people receive the same diagnosis, their experiences can vastly differ. In sharing the Mardon's story we hope to work towards the de-stigmatization of mental illness and add more real representations of what it's like to live with a mental illness and be in a relationship.

CHAPTER 1
Searching for Acceptance

Austin recalls experiencing symptoms of schizophrenia as early as 1985 but wasn't officially diagnosed until 1992 at the age of 30. According to the World Health Organization (2019) 20 million people worldwide have schizophrenia, though it's unknown what the exact cause is (it may be a combination of genes, environment, and psychosocial factors). Symptoms of schizophrenia may include but are not limited to, hallucinations, delusions, disorganized behavior, disconnect of emotions, and difficulty understanding facial expressions or body language. Because Austin's mom had schizophrenia, growing up he was well aware of the disorder and it's symptoms but, for a long time, he refused to acknowledge any of the signs that he had it too. Symptoms he can recognize now, but refused to accept then, were irrationality, paranoia, ineptitude to read body language, and inability to understand the why behind people's behavior. His actions were erratic and didn't make logical sense to others. For example, he used the resources meant for his PhD to publish a book of his dad's rather than complete his doctorate program like he was supposed to. In 1992 he had his first major episode where he experienced delusions and hallucinations. This was the turning point that forced him to realize he needed to accept his diagnosis. Austin didn't fear schizophrenia itself the way others might because he had experienced it all alongside his mom. Instead, he feared the loss of opportunity that a diagnosis would mean for him. For years he had been bullied physically and mentally by classmates because of his mother's illness. He believed a diagnosis would change how people saw him which would affect his ability to access further education and a career in academics. The discrimination Austin feared was and continues to be a challenge for people with any kind of disability. Schizophrenia is a fairly rare mental illness compared to other more common ones like depression or anxiety, so there's even greater stigma and misunderstanding surrounding it. Even after the diagnosis, he was in denial and it took a lot of effort for him to begin to accept his schizophrenia. There are treatments, including medication and therapy, that can lessen the symptoms of schizophrenia but there's currently no cure. Austin has now learned to accept his diagnosis and chooses to openly share, educate, and be an advocate for himself and others who have schizophrenia.

Although Austin had personally accepted his schizophrenia, as he predicted, there were a lot of people who treated him poorly because of it. Austin shared that there were two ways people regularly reacted to hearing his diagnosis: either they believed he should be hospitalized or they believed he was malingering and should get a full-time job. When he was diagnosed, he was told by doctors at the hospital that he would likely be homeless, his life was over, and that he was better off dead. They told him they couldn't help him. Austin was kicked out of his PhD program and laughed at when he applied for others. When he was properly recognized for his various academic and activist achievements, including hundreds of publications and a PhD in geography, his family was embarrassed. Prestige was important to his dad's side of the family and they were upset that their name was being tied to schizophrenia in the newspapers, despite that it was due to Austin's many accomplishments and awards.

Austin had proven wrong the people who said his life was over after his diagnosis, but he still yearned for something more. Children and marriage were something Austin knew he wanted both before and after his diagnosis. When he shared this hope with others, he was met with further skepticism and malicious comments. He was told by several people that he should be sterilized because he was a genetic defect. Some of the people who said these horrible things were medical professionals - psychiatrists, doctors, and nurses. Stigma was and continues to be a battle for Austin, as it is for many people who have schizophrenia and other mental health conditions. Austin has found the stigma has lessened throughout the years and credits the LGBTQ2S+ community for pushing for greater social acceptance and paving the way for other groups, like people with mental illnesses. Although this improvement is true, there is still a lot of work that needs to be done. A study looking at UN countries found that "in 37% (71 countries) laws explicitly prohibit marriage by persons with mental health problems," and many of these laws use "non-scientific, derogatory, and archaic terminology" (Bhugra et al., 2016, p. 388). There continues to be blatant discrimination against people who have mental health conditions and it's ingrained in the very institute of marriage.

Healthy relationships and connections can help people and their mental health; no matter the disability, everyone deserves love. Every night Austin prayed that he would find love and be able to have kids, then cry himself to sleep, believing it was unattainable.

Three thousand kilometers south of Austin, in the United States, Catherine Curry was facing her own mental health challenges. In 1991 Catherine was working as a lawyer in Oklahoma when she became entangled in the investigation of a white supremacist group. She was attacked by one of their members who stabbed her 17 times and pushed her down a flight of stairs. Catherine sustained a brain injury and nerve damage along with several other physical injuries that caused her to be confined to a wheelchair. This violent attack also eventually led to her being diagnosed with Post-Traumatic Stress Disorder (PTSD) in 1996. It's estimated that 1 in 11 people will be diagnosed with Post Traumatic Stress Disorder in their lifetime (American Psychiatric Association, 2020). PTSD is triggered by experiencing or witnessing a traumatic event which causes symptoms that last long after the event occurred. The symptoms can include intrusive thoughts or flashbacks, avoiding triggers that are reminders of the event, distorted thoughts and feelings, being overly reactive, or having difficulty sleeping. Similarly to Austin, Catherine refused to acknowledge her symptoms. The most noticeable of them was avoidance. She avoided stairs because of where the attack had taken place and she hid from any situation that could potentially lead to strong emotions. Whether those were good or bad emotions, it didn't matter. She couldn't handle being congratulated, being in a crowd, dealing with angry or excited people, or loud noises. Due to this, she began to isolate herself into smaller and smaller spaces until she didn't engage with anyone about anything. She also began experiencing flashbacks of the attack and nightmares. Because of where and when it happened, she wasn't eligible for worker's compensation or insurance to help cover the medical costs and rehabilitation for her physical injuries, let alone her mental scars. Catherine was so focused on her physical recovery and attempting to hide her brain injury from her job, that she wouldn't even entertain the thought that she might have PTSD. She compared the experience of attempting to hide all of her symptoms to being a juggler, having a bunch of balls in the air and continually adding more, until, inevitably, they all fall. Hiding symptoms, whether of a mental illness or a disability, can be exhausting. Similar to Austin, Catherine was scared of what admitting something was wrong would mean. She pretended she was fine but her symptoms soon became too noticeable to hide at work and she was told she could either medically retire or would face a competency hearing. She couldn't stand the thought of being publicly outed, so she retired. They allowed her to keep her license as long as she didn't try any court cases. Instead, she began volunteering as a lawyer for people with disabilities who were trying to get their pensions.

Three or four years after the attack Catherine was mistakenly diagnosed with schizophrenia. She didn't have health insurance at the time so was being treated by students and they weren't able to distinguish that the voices she was hearing were actually flashbacks rather than hallucinations. It hadn't occurred to her that it might actually be post-traumatic stress disorder because the only people she knew who lived with it were her father and other veterans. She assumed only the experience of war could cause PTSD. Three or four years after that she was properly diagnosed with PTSD and began taking medication that helped with her nightmares, panic attacks, and flashbacks. A few years later she began receiving therapy for her PTSD as well. There are still certain triggers for her, but she has learned to cope with and accept her diagnosis. She also continues to be affected by the traumatic brain injury. She developed partial aphasia, the loss of the ability to produce language, meaning her brain often mixes up words. For example, she could be shown a pencil, know it's a pencil but still might call it a banana. As the day goes on the aphasia often worsens and she becomes more and more fatigued. Although Catherine has dealt with a lot of challenges due to her diagnosis, she's found she faced less stigma than people with other disorders because she was more easily able to hide hers. For a long time, she just didn't tell anyone about it, not even her family, because she feared being judged. She has since learned to accept all of her disabilities and be an advocate for herself and others.

Unlike Austin, Catherine hadn't thought much about kids and marriage because she'd always been too busy to worry about it. Catherine was the youngest child in her family. There was a 19 year age gap between her and her oldest brother and because of this, she grew up babysitting all of her nieces and nephews. By the time she was old enough to have kids, she didn't want to change any more diapers or have kids of her own. Catherine always had children in her life though. She took care of her teenage nephew for a while and, after she was injured, she fostered a 3-year-old boy and then his brother as well. The boys' mom was a friend of Catherine's but had a history of mental illness and was not well enough to take care of them. Catherine had always thought that these boys would be enough of a family for her. However, when both boys were grown and out of the house, she was able to begin truly taking care of herself for the first time in a long time. This gave her the opportunity to begin thinking about what she really wanted and she realized that for her that included marriage and kids.

Experiencing a mental illness can be extremely isolating. Austin and Catherine both struggled to come to terms with their new reality and what their diagnosis would mean for their future. They each faced stigma and discrimination as they tried to advocate for themselves. As they began learning to accept their diagnoses, they also began searching for someone else who might accept and understand them as well.

CHAPTER 2

Meeting & Disclosing

Austin and Catherine met in 2005 via the dating website Ave Maria. To join the website, you had to be intentionally seeking marriage and believe in the teachings of the Catholic church. Faith was a large part of both Austin and Catherine's lives and each of them felt called to the vocation of marriage. Austin boasts it was Catherine who showed interest first by sending the first message. Coincidently, a few weeks prior, Catherine had been waiting in a psychiatrist's office for her friend and happened to pick up a Schizophrenia Digest magazine. Ever the sports fan, she was reading an article about a football player while an article about Austin happened to be on the next page. She noted his picture, but didn't have time to read further. Later, while scrolling through Ave Maria, she noticed Austin's picture and having felt like she'd seen him somewhere before she decided to message him. They'd find out months later that the article where Austin talked about the isolating experience of having schizophrenia and wishing to have someone to share his life with, was the reason Catherine recognized him. Unfortunately, Austin was away on holidays the first time Catherine messaged him so he wasn't regularly checking his profile. A week passed with no reply and Catherine wrote him off, assuming he wasn't interested. When Austin logged onto his profile the next week at a local library and saw the message from Catherine he could hardly contain his excitement and replied immediately. Catherine still teases him about making her wait and almost missing out on the opportunity to meet.

Austin and Catherine soon began exchanging long messages. They sent page after page of emails to each other. When the length of Catherine's emails neared 30 pages at a time Austin decided he couldn't keep up and it was time he purchased a data plan so they could talk on the phone. The first time he called he was so nervous he said hello, goodbye, and immediately hung up. At least this time it didn't take him a week to reply. He emailed her right after to apologize and create more of a conversation. Catherine however was just as chatty over the phone as she was in her emails. More than once Austin fell asleep while talking on the phone with her. Catherine didn't notice until his snores drowned her out. They continued their long distance relationship like this for the next three months.

For many people, meeting someone new is stressful. That stress is often multiplied and complicated when someone has a mental illness. There can be pressure to hide it which causes anxiety or fear about being upfront and open about it. Afraid his admission of having schizophrenia would send Catherine running like it had for people in the past, Austin was hesitant to tell her. Rather than initiating the conversation himself, Austin planned to convince Catherine to look him up online where she would inevitably stumble upon an article about him that mentioned his schizophrenia. At that point, Austin had made quite a name for himself in academia and mental health activism. Many of the articles written about him discussed his schizophrenia diagnosis. Hopeful Catherine would find one of these, saving him from having to initiate the conversation, Austin continually dropped hints that he wanted Catherine to Google search him. At first she didn't want to but, eventually, she succumbed to curiosity. To Austin's dismay she never found any articles mentioning his schizophrenia. Eventually Austin decided if he wanted their relationship to continue he'd have to tell Catherine about his schizophrenia. When he finally told her, she asked whether he was on medication and planning to stay on it. Austin answered an honest yes to both questions, to which Catherine replied "Ok, so what?" Austin couldn't believe it! No one had ever responded like that and he didn't know what to make of it. Thinking maybe she didn't know what schizophrenia was he tried to explain what it would actually mean to date him. She explained she had quite a bit of experience working with people who had schizophrenia and as long as he consistently took his medication she was fine with it. It was different from any of his past experiences. Unlike so many others, she didn't judge him based on his diagnosis, she was understanding and accepted every part of him. Catherine then proceeded to tell him about her brain injury, physical disabilities, and PTSD from the attack and he too was accepting of all parts of her.

Not everyone's experience of disclosing a mental illness goes as seamlessly as Austin and Catherine's. Knowing how and when to tell someone you're dating about your diagnosis is difficult. Sometimes it can feel easier to avoid telling them, but even when symptoms are more easily hidden like Catherine's were, it can eventually affect you and the relationship. Austin knew he had to tell Catherine about his schizophrenia partly because he knew she'd find out eventually, and partly because it would be necessary for them to have a future together. A blog from the National Alliance on Mental Illness suggests making a disclosure when you feel comfortable and well, rather than waiting until you're having trouble and need more support (Tubbs, 2019). It's true that sometimes it's possible to plan when to make a disclosure, but that's not always the case. A partner may notice symptoms and ask, or there may be a time when you need to tell them because you need extra support. Tubbs (2019) also recommends waiting until you're comfortable enough to share and even then only sharing what you're ready to. Waiting awhile until you know someone better to make a disclosure, like Austin did, is okay. When he knew he wanted a serious long term relationship with Catherine he told her about his schizophrenia. Not everyone will react the way Catherine did, some people may need to take more time to process. It can take time, questions and further education for someone to understand. When Catherine and Austin met, online dating was still fairly new, but it's become much more common. Now there are even dating websites specifically made for people with mental illnesses. This can help take the pressure off of disclosing because everyone on the website has experience of living with some form of mental health challenge.

With everything now out in the open, Austin and Catherine were able to continue getting to know each other. After three months of talking long distance, they decided to meet in person. They planned to meet in October, but Catherine wasn't a huge fan of flying and wasn't able to get a cheap plane ticket on such short notice. Instead she decided to take a bus from St.Petersburg, Florida to where Austin lived in Edmonton, Alberta. The trip took five days. In the beginning, the bus ride was overwhelming for Catherine. She'd lived sheltered and secluded for several years due to her PTSD and had grown used to avoiding crowds and loud places. Yet she persevered because she was determined to meet Austin.

At each stop Catherine was intrigued by the people filling the already crowded bus, from a family of Mennonites to a group of prisoners. Somewhat distracted by people watching, the bus ride got slightly better but the overnight stops were dreadful. Catherine shudders as she recalls their stop in Nebraska. The next bus wasn't scheduled to arrive until morning so they had no choice but to stay overnight at the bus stop. The rest stop had a convenience store attached to it so the group of bus-riders grabbed a booth and sat together. By this point, it was about 3:00am. Exhausted, they couldn't resist putting their heads on the table to sleep for a few minutes. They were jolted awake by a man banging on the table and yelling that they weren't allowed to sleep there. The remainder of the night was spent running outside into the frigid cold air to keep themselves awake. Another night on her trip, Catherine had to sleep in the lineup for the bus in order to save her spot. When she was younger, she often travelled by bus to South America. During these trips she'd sleep in the bus lines on her duffel bag but she hadn't done this in years. At this point she'd only been walking for six months, having spent the previous eight years in a wheelchair due to the injuries from her attack. Since relearning to walk Catherine had never had to get down to the ground and back up. She wasn't even sure if she could. She'd been awake for nearly 48 hours because of the loud noises and bright lights on the bus and sleeping standing up wasn't an option, so she didn't have a choice. Eventually, she mustered up the courage to lay down and decided she could wake someone to ask for help getting up if she needed. The next morning Catherine got up without assistance. This was a powerful moment on her recovery journey as she realized she could still do the things she'd done before the attack. The trip wasn't over yet, though. There were more roadblocks when she reached the Canadian border. The officials were hesitant to allow her into the country, as they asked a lot of questions about why she was there and who she was going to meet. She called Austin to help explain their story. Austin told them they had met through internet dating and the border agents couldn't believe it. They thought it was a terrible way to meet someone. Some of Austin's friends had felt the same way, believing a proper woman wouldn't put herself on the internet that way. Of course, nowadays, internet dating is incredibly common but at that time it was fairly new and still carried a lot of stigma which only added to the stigma they already faced with having mental illnesses.

Both Catherine and Austin were anxious about meeting. They shared similar insecurities, each believed the other would take one look at them and leave. They were afraid their physical appearance wouldn't live up to the other person's expectation. When Catherine's bus was scheduled to arrive Austin showed up at the bus depot with flowers. An hour went by, then another, and another, until he'd been waiting for four hours. The friend who had driven him there assumed Austin was having delusions and that there was never a woman named Catherine coming from Florida to meet him. She was proven wrong when Catherine did in fact show up, albeit four hours late and near delirious from exhaustion. Despite their fears, neither of them bolted upon seeing the other, and they decided to go on their first date right then.

CHAPTER 3

Dating & Discrimination

Although it was nearing 2am, Catherine and Austin were eager to get to know each other and go on a real date. It was Thanksgiving weekend so the only place open after midnight was an Alcoholics Anonymous clubhouse called KISS - Keep It Simple Stupid. While Austin and Catherine chatted over turkey dinner they found they had a lot of similar interests. They liked the same books and movies, and rarely ran out of things to talk about. Austin was impressed by Catherine's intelligence and how much she knew about meteorites and the Treaty of Versailles. If he had been unsure at all, he knew right then she was definitely a keeper. Catherine planned to stay in Canada for a month and because Austin had recently lost his job they were able to spend almost the entire time together. As they spent more time together they began to learn about each other and each other's mental illnesses. For the first two weeks Catherine was in Edmonton, Austin wouldn't let her near his house. Warning bells sounded in her mind. When he finally agreed to show her his house she had no idea what to expect but it definitely wasn't this. There were books and papers everywhere, even in the stove! They covered nearly every surface in the house. Austin was a bit of a hoarder, and cleaning and cooking were two things she realized she'd have to teach him. Catherine wondered how he had lived on his own this long without blowing himself up. She didn't scare easily though, she accepted these were things they could work on together.

As Austin introduced Catherine to his friends and family, the couple faced a lot of skepticism. Catherine was interrogated by almost everyone she met in Edmonton. She was staying with an older woman from Austin's church and when she returned that first night the woman kept her up until nearly five in the morning. She grilled Catherine on how she grew up, where she went to school, how many siblings she had, and on and on and on. Later, when Catherine met Austin's pastor, he did the same. The first question for Catherine was always if she had schizophrenia. When she told them no, they continued their investigation, figuring she must have a different mental illness. At first Catherine chalked it up to people being protective of Austin but she now thinks that people are just horribly curious. Having schizophrenia is one thing but marrying someone who has schizophrenia seems to blow everyone's minds. They thought something had to be wrong with her. When some people learned of Catherine's brain injury, they reasoned she must have some kind of deficit and that was why she was willingly dating Austin. Austin was upset people couldn't fathom how a 'normal' person could be in love with him. They treated him as though he were unlovable. Some people don't see past Austin's diagnosis, they think of him as a schizophrenic person, rather than a person who has schizophrenia along with a lot of other qualities. Austin blames the continued negative perception of schizophrenia that reinforces the negative view he has of himself. Because so many people see Austin this way, he sometimes doubts himself and the good qualities he has, but Catherine is always quick to remind him of all the things she loves about him.

Although mental health has become a more common topic, it continues to carry a lot of stigma. A Canadian survey conducted in 2014 found that one third of people who experienced a mental health challenge felt they were treated unfairly by family, romantic partners, school, or work, because of it (Stuart, Patten, Koller, Modgill, & Liinamaa, 2014, p. S31). Of the people surveyed, 33% thought people would not date someone who has depression, and 20% thought people would not accept a friend who has depression (Stuart, Patten, Koller, Modgill, & Liinamaa, 2014, p. S29). The study suggests there is a negative stigma towards people who have lived experience of a mental illness as well as self-stigma they may place upon themselves. Austin believing he doesn't have any good qualities because of his schizophrenia is an example of self-stigma. Often self-stigma is influenced by external stigma, in Austin's case, people reducing him to only his diagnosis.

Prior to meeting Catherine, Austin dated a woman who wanted him to work full time. He tried to explain his schizophrenia and how for him working full time wasn't a possibility, but she just didn't understand. He appreciated Catherine all the more because she understood his limitations while also realizing his strengths. Austin was also married once before Catherine to a woman who had schizophrenia. It was a challenging marriage for various reasons and Austin thought a lot about the mistakes he made in that marriage before dating someone else. He decided he was open to dating someone with a mental illness, but it would complicate things too much for him if they had schizophrenia. Not everyone who has a mental health challenge shares Austin's feelings. Nordsletten et al (2016) found there may be patterns of mating across psychological disorders, meaning people with a psychological disorder are more likely to romantically be with someone who also has a disorder. For certain disorders people may have an even higher likelihood of being with someone who has that same disorder (Nordsletten et al, 2016). It's unknown exactly why this is but, it could be because people feel the other person has a better understanding of what it's like to live with a mental illness. Austin and Catherine share this belief and appreciate each other's shared experiences.

Introducing a significant other to the family can be an important step in a relationship. Unfortunately, it doesn't always go smoothly and it definitely didn't for Austin and Catherine. Saying Austin's family wasn't thrilled with his new relationship is an understatement. They tried to sabotage it multiple times and this continued escalating when Catherine arrived in Edmonton. Catherine was taken aback by their interference. It never would've occurred to her to treat someone the way they treated her. They weren't able to give Austin a concrete reason as to why they were so upset by his relationship, for whatever reason they just didn't like Catherine. Catherine believes that sometimes when people interfere in others' lives, they tell themselves they're trying to protect them or do what's best for them. She thought maybe this was how Austin's family justified what they were doing. Some of the family believed Catherine had an ulterior motive for dating Austin. They told him she must be on the run from the law or after his money. When they weren't able to prove any of these theories they continued trying to interfere in other ways. At times it was as though they were battling Catherine because they wanted control of Austin. Austin thinks because of his schizophrenia his family sometimes forgot he was an adult capable of making his own decisions. Infantilizing people who have a mental illness or other disability is common. Family members and significant others should instead support their agency and ability to make their own choices. Catherine differed from Austin's family in this way, she treated him as an equal partner capable of making his own decisions.

Catherine's mother wasn't thrilled about the relationship either. She had moved to Florida to be nearer to Catherine where she could help take care of her as she got older. She thought Catherine would stay there so when she learned of her boyfriend who lived in Canada, she was worried Catherine would abandon her. It wasn't that Catherine didn't want to take care of her, she just didn't think they could live that closely without killing each other. Catherine and her mom had a complicated relationship and got along best when they lived further apart. Her mother's concern about Austin also stemmed from her own past experience. Her first husband experienced psychosis while fighting in the Korean war. He disappeared from battle in Korea and was found weeks later wandering the streets of Tokyo, not knowing who or where he was. The army wouldn't admit he had a mental illness. Instead they claimed he was a deserter and her mom had to fight to get him discharged and brought home. When he came back he went straight to the hospital and was diagnosed with schizophrenia. That was before there was proper medication or treatment for schizophrenia, so he had a very difficult time dealing with it. It was common for veterans like him who returned from the war to not receive the proper help they needed. Many struggled to reintegrate back into society after the trauma they had experienced. He pushed Catherine's mom out of a moving car when she was six months pregnant which caused her to lose the child. Then he spent fifteen years in and out of hospitals until Catherine's mother divorced him and he later died by suicide. Due to the violent experiences she had with him, Catherine's mom was frightened of people who had schizophrenia. She was afraid Austin would hurt Catherine and didn't trust that Catherine fully realized what she was getting herself into. Catherine's mom isn't the only one with this belief. There's a misconception that people with mental illness, in particular schizophrenia, are dangerous or violent. Catherine argues that most people who have schizophrenia aren't dangerous at all and that a lot of them are like Austin, scared of his own shadow. People who have schizophrenia are actually more likely to be victims of a crime or a danger to themselves. A study from the UK found psychiatric patients "were five times more likely to be victims of assault" than the general population (Khalifeh et al., 2015, p. 280). Studies in Ontario have shown 1 in 10 suicide deaths are people with schizophrenia (Centre for Addictions and Mental Health, 2018). It's clear schizophrenia is a very misunderstood illness and people who live with it need better support. Austin had been on his medication for about twenty years when he and Catherine began dating. He hadn't once gone off it so Catherine didn't have any concerns about his schizophrenia. Eventually Catherine's mom warmed up to Austin and they developed a strong relationship. Austin often talked to her on the phone, even more than Catherine did. The rest of Catherine's family wasn't very involved with or concerned by her relationship with Austin. She was a lot younger than all of her brothers so they weren't that close. They were all busy with their own kids and jobs so most of the news they heard about each other came from talking to their mom. When her closest brother heard about her dating Austin he joked the family was happy to finally be getting rid of her.

Catherine and Austin faced a lot of skepticism and stigma from the beginning of their relationship. A lot of friends' and families' concerns stemmed from the fact that Austin had schizophrenia. Fear and apprehension can come with misunderstanding a mental illness. Clearly, there continues to be a lot of work that needs to be done towards spreading factual information. A diagnosis doesn't mean a person is incompetent or unable to make their own decisions, including choosing who to love. It also needs to be recognized that people who have any kind of disability or mental illness are capable and worthy of love.

CHAPTER 4

I Do

Austin proposed to Catherine after only two weeks of her being in Edmonton. The woman Catherine had been staying with had been pressuring Austin to propose from the first night she got there. Knowing Catherine would be gone at the end of the month, she told him if Catherine got back on that bus he'd never see her again. One night Catherine made a key lime pie for the woman as a hostess gift. Key lime pie is very rich, similar to cheesecake, so Catherine only served each of them a small piece. Austin got up to get himself another piece, returned from the kitchen with the entire pie pan, and proceeded to eat the whole remaining pie. The woman chuckled to Catherine 'you've got him now'. Later that night their host went to church, leaving Austin and Catherine alone. Austin looked at Catherine and blurted, 'well I suppose we should get married'. Catherine just stared at him dumbfounded. She knew what she was getting with Austin - it wasn't like she had expected an extravagant proposal or sweeping declaration of love but this wasn't what she'd hoped for either. She demanded that if he didn't get on one knee and ask her properly she'd make him call her brother to ask for permission. Never before or since has she seen Austin move so fast. The very next day the newly engaged couple went to pick out a ring. Catherine didn't want a traditional diamond ring. She informed Austin it would just get in the way when she used her beloved power tools. Austin loved her even more in that moment because she wasn't concerned about expensive material possessions, she just wanted him. Together they picked out a simple silver claddagh ring. A claddagh ring is a traditional Irish ring with a heart being held by two hands and a crown sitting on top. It signifies love, loyalty, and friendship, a fitting symbol for their relationship.

As shocking as an engagement after only knowing each other for three months is, Austin and Catherine were certain they wanted to spend the rest of their lives together. It wasn't as though they were 20 year olds anymore, as Catherine says, their bones were already half gone to dust. Both felt they were mature enough to know marriage was a commitment they were ready to make. The website they met on is specifically for devout Catholics who are called to the vocation of marriage, so they had both discerned they wanted to marry even before signing up. Catherine and Austin agree marriage is difficult no matter who you are or what your circumstances are, whether you have a mental illness or not. They both believed they had found someone who was willing to do whatever it took to make a marriage work and last.

Part of this included understanding the challenges that might come with being married to someone who had a mental illness. Austin felt Catherine understood what it meant to marry someone who had schizophrenia and was willing to go along the journey with him and be his partner. Catherine's view was that even if she married someone who was perfectly healthy, they could become injured or develop a mental illness at any time. For her it's about choosing to be with each other through rich and poor, sickness and in health. She believes the main difference between marriages that last fifty years and those that don't is people understanding marriage is forever; it's being willing to do the work it takes. Being married to someone with a mental illness isn't always easy but, being married to anyone isn't always easy. No one is perfect, so you'll never find a perfect person to marry. Austin and Catherine think maybe they knew from their first meeting they wanted to spend the rest of their lives together, but it's also something they rediscover every day. They choose to be with each other on the sunny days and the rainy ones. Growing up, Catherine had two aunts who she described as the nice one and the mean one. Both had long marriages. The mean one's husband worked out of town and only came home on weekends, while the nice aunt married a man who didn't make much money, but they were very happy together. The latter did a lot of activities together like golfing and bowling. From watching her aunts she learned that you have to do what it takes to make a marriage work, it's important to make time to do activities you enjoy together, and money doesn't buy happiness. She believes her and Austin strive to practice both aunts' teachings.

Although Austin and Catherine were excited about their engagement, some of their families and friends weren't quite as enthusiastic. They planned to have their civil marriage ceremony three months after their engagement. The church wedding was scheduled to happen later, but they needed to be legally married for Catherine to be permitted to live in Canada. The ceremony was to take place at Austin's sister's house but the day before it was supposed to happen Austin's sister cancelled it. No reason was given, she just refused to have them married there. Scrambling to find a location on such short notice, the only option they could think of was their hotel room. They happened to be booked at the fantasyland hotel in the Roman themed room - an interesting wedding venue to say the least. Everyone was ordered to sneak into the hotel room quietly because if staff realized there was a party they'd be charged extra. It wasn't what Catherine and Austin were expecting but it was certainly memorable.

With their civil union complete and Catherine safe from deportation for the time being, the couple prepared for their Catholic wedding. To be allowed to get married in the Catholic church Austin and Catherine needed to complete a marriage preparation program. Part of that was meeting with the priest and other couples. Catherine and Austin found it a bit awkward because the other couples were clearly a lot younger than them. Austin was triggered by the uncomfortable situation and it made him anxious and paranoid. Catherine helped to reassure him and together they made it through premarital counselling. They thought they were ready to officially marry but yet again their wedding plans were disrupted by Austin's family. Two days before the wedding Austin's sister called their priest claiming Austin had gone off his schizophrenia medication and was abusing Catherine. Of course this wasn't true but, being a fairly inexperienced priest and not knowing the family or couple well, he couldn't imagine why someone would lie about that. Catherine and Austin both having a psychological disorder also played a factor in the conclusions the priest drew. They both had to get letters from their doctors saying their diagnoses and Catherine's brain injury didn't affect their capacity to consent to marriage. The misconception that having a mental illness means an inability to make certain decisions continues to be an issue. There are many laws that discourage people who have a mental illness from being married. In 6% of UN countries, people with mental illnesses are only allowed to marry after they receive approval from a family member and in some countries approval from an expert or institution (Bhugra, 2016, p. 388). In Austin's case, his family likely would've declined which would mean he couldn't marry Catherine even though he has the capacity to consent.

The wedding was postponed until Catherine and Austin attended another three months of premarital counselling along with their doctors' notes. This time the priest wanted them to complete it at Catholic Social Services with a registered psychologist to ensure they were able to make the commitment of marriage. To enter into the sacrament of marriage in the Catholic church it needs to be ensured that both parties are mature enough, understand marriage is a lifelong commitment, and neither is being pressured into it. The priest was sending them to a registered psychologist to ensure each of them was of 'sound mind' and able to consent. It took them two months to get an appointment with a counsellor who was Catholic and would complete their counselling for free. At the time they were struggling financially because Austin's family had left them without a home, Catherine was still paying rent in St. Petersburg until her lease was up, and she was also needing to pay for health insurance because she wasn't yet covered in Canada. When they were finally able to get an appointment, they arrived, filled out the paperwork, and sat down with the counsellor. The first thing she brought up was Ausin's schizophrenia. The couple tensed, waiting for the bombardment of questions about his mental state, but they never came. The counselor asked if Austin was on medication, to which he replied yes. She then asked if he planned to stay on his medication, to which he again replied yes. The counsellor wrote a note, declared he was fine, and basically shoved them out the door. Austin and Catherine were relieved but panicked. It likely wasn't exactly what the priest had in mind when he requested they receive counselling. At this point nearly everything that could possibly go wrong had, but Austin and Catherine continued to persevere.

By this time their priest had talked to another priest who knew Austin's family better and confirmed they were in fact capable of lying about such things. He had also spoken to Catherine's brother from Oklahoma. The priest asked questions about whether she was married before and if she was running from something. Austin's family had told the priest Catherine was a criminal which was why she was escaping to Canada. She'd already completed various background checks to be allowed to immigrate so that wasn't likely but the priest had to be thorough. Austin's family also claimed she was desperate to have a baby and that was why they got married so quickly. Her brother laughed when he heard the accusation. He didn't think Catherine was even born with a biological clock. When asked if Catherine had ever been married before he joked 'No, but we sure tried hard to get rid of her.' The priest was reassured by Catherine's brother and by this time he'd also gotten to know Catherine better. No longer believing Austin's family's lies, he agreed to marry them.

Perhaps he felt bad for what they had gone through because the priest got special permission from the bishop to marry them in the church on a Sunday. This wasn't typically allowed. On Sunday at 7am Austin and Catherine arrived at the church with a couple of close friends. Rather than letting them in through the front the priest had them go through the rectory and the hallway that connects to the church while keeping the front doors locked. Maybe he thought Austin's family would barge in for one final attempt to stop the wedding. Two friends of Catherine's were late though and were locked out. They were pounding on the church door to be let in, but the priest wouldn't stop the ceremony, thinking it really was Austin's family trying to interrupt. The priest spoke as fast as an auctioneer, trying to complete the ceremony before they broke the door down. Catherine had just recovered from laryngitis so she could barely speak her vows above a whisper. Meanwhile Austin had a plugged ear from the shower that morning so he was yelling his. It was the strangest whirlwind of a wedding. A non-Catholic friend asked if this was what all Catholic weddings were like because they were a lot more exciting than he thought they'd be. It was a lot more exciting than Austin and Catherine had planned it to be. Although they faced a lot of challenges on the road to getting married, they were determined, and finally officially became the Mardons.

CHAPTER 5

Making Adjustments

After they were married in January of 2006, the Mardons decided Catherine would move to Edmonton Alberta. They came to this conclusion mainly because of finances. Catherine's main income was her social security pension from the states which she would be able to receive no matter where she moved. Austin's main income was AISH - Assured Income for the Severely Handicapped, which would've stopped at the Alberta border. If he were to move to the US with Catherine, he also would've had to start paying for health insurance and his schizophrenia medication which was very expensive. Even though it was the logical choice, it was a difficult decision to make, especially for Catherine. She was sad to be leaving the place she'd begun to call home and the warm Florida weather, but was excited to start a new life with Austin. When Catherine arrived in Edmonton she went to set up a bank account and was chatting with the bank teller. The teller couldn't believe she'd willingly moved from St. Petersburg to Edmonton in January, the dead of Canadian winter. When Catherine insisted she had, the teller laughed and said 'There must be a man involved!'

When they moved in together there were a lot of discoveries and adjustments to be made. Austin had been living as a bachelor for a long time and Catherine had never been married so living with someone else was a new experience for both of them. Catherine likened moving in with Austin to an archaeological expedition. They spent weeks going through his papers and books which covered nearly every surface in the house, including some shoved inside the oven. It also turned into a bit of a treasure hunt as they began to find loose change under all the cushions and in every corner. They found $1500 in change which Catherine used to pay her immigration fees. Catherine's organizational style was a big change for Austin, but he wasn't upset because he was happy to be working towards a more liveable space for the both of them. He actually quite enthusiastically got into the spirit of cleaning. One week he stayed up for two or three nights to go through all of his old papers, deciding which ones to keep and which to get rid of. Eager to help in any way he could, Catherine was shocked to learn he hadn't been taught a lot of basic cleaning skills. When he helped she had to explain everything to him and show him how to do it. Catherine and Austin quickly realized it was best if Catherine did the majority of the household chores because she was too particular about how things were done. Austin did a few things around the house but his main responsibility was taking his medication every day. Household chores were never really an argument for Austin and Catherine but it can be for a lot of couples. It can also become more complex when mental health challenges are involved. Depending where someone is in their wellness, they may have difficulties with household tasks. Someone who has depression may have periods when just getting out of bed and taking care of themself is all they have energy for. This might mean more household responsibilities fall on their partner. Someone with Obsessive Compulsive Disorder on the other hand, might be very particular about how things are done and won't let someone else rearrange or clean their space. It's important to communicate how you feel and be understanding of where your partner is at.

Austin and Catherine planned to continue living in the house Austin currently lived in and had purchased years before. However, they soon found out that when he bought it, it hadn't been put in his name. Even though he'd made the down payment and mortgage payments, his realtor, who was a family member, had placed it in the family's name rather than his. His family threatened to sell the house if Catherine continued living with him so they had no option but to find somewhere else to live. Austin felt embarrassed that he'd been taken advantage of by his family. He felt guilty that Catherine had given up her country and family and was now living in a strange place where she didn't know anyone and didn't even have a place to live. He became paranoid that he would die of a heart attack or his family would put him in a psychiatric ward, making Catherine homeless and alone. The stress and shame he felt began to manifest in serious physical chest pain. Catherine reassured him she was just happy to share a life with him, they didn't need an expensive house.

Although they moved out of Austin's old house, his family still didn't accept their relationship and continued trying to break them up. His mom attempted to have Catherine deported by telling their local Member of Parliament that Catherine had snuck into the country and was an eco-terrorist. Because of this Catherine had to endure checks from the RCMP and FBI that went way beyond the normal process of becoming a permanent resident of Canada. When Catherine was about two weeks away from getting deported, Austin decided they had no choice but to call his connection at the RCMP to help. Austin had met him through the schizophrenia society when his son was diagnosed. Luckily, he was able to straighten out the misunderstanding. It should've only taken Catherine four to six months to become a permanent resident of Canada but it ended up taking her sixteen months. When Catherine was no longer being threatened with deportation, Austin's mom tried to convince him that Catherine only married him so she could get her permanent residency. When Catherine was granted permanent residency and still stuck around, Austin's mom told him Catherine would only stay until she was a Canadian citizen. Again, the supposed deadline came and went but Catherine stayed. His mom couldn't understand why Catherine was still there. She then resorted to telling Austin Catherine was going to divorce him and steal everything from him. She called Catherine his 'second wife' or 'it', never by her name. It was hurtful to both Austin and Catherine that his family would try so hard to separate them. Despite his family's continued attempts, Catherine and Austin held strong together.

Similar to Austin's mom, a lot of people who met the Mardons assumed Catherine must have some ulterior motive for marrying him. People thought it was impossible that someone seemingly 'normal' would choose to marry someone who had schizophrenia. Austin was hurt by this because it felt like they couldn't understand how someone like him was capable of being loved. Some people think so poorly of people who have mental health conditions they thought it was impossible to marry someone that had schizophrenia. Even the archbishop looked at Catherine like she was doing some great sacrifice by being married to Austin. As a couple they faced a lot of push back from other people and this was hard on them; it made it feel like it was them against everyone else.

Catherine also carried her own guilt about their relationship. Despite not having done anything wrong, she felt bad she'd come between Austin and his family. Catherine always offered to take him to spend time with his family even if she wasn't on good terms with them. She wanted him to be able to maintain his relationship with them if he wanted to, regardless of how she felt about them. Austin also lost some friends because of his marriage. Before meeting Catherine, he was often the person in groups who was bullied or made fun of. Austin had been bullied growing up and had become so accustomed to being treated this way by his friends that he almost thought it was normal. When he married Catherine she didn't tell him who he could and couldn't hangout with but she wouldn't let them call him names or treat him poorly like they had in the past. Catherine thought some of Austin's friends made fun of him because their families or friends treated them badly, complaining that they didn't have a job or live on their own. Taking their emotions out on Austin helped with this. They couldn't understand why Austin had a wife and they didn't so making fun of him was a way to make themselves feel better. When she no longer let them do this, a lot of them left. Even though they weren't great friends to Austin, Catherine felt horrible that he had lost friends because of her, particularly the ones who left immediately just at the idea of her. The upside to the situation was Austin found out who his true friends were.

Although Austin had parted ways with some friends he continued to be a very social person. According to Catherine he was always a gregarious man. He needed to constantly be talking on the phone or having guests over. Catherine being a lot quieter and less social had to adjust to it. One day after church Austin had a friend over and Catherine made pancakes for them. She made the mistake of telling Austin she'd made too many because the next thing she knew their whole house was full of people! After church pancakes quickly became a weekly tradition which then turned into the Mardons hosting parties nearly every holiday for anyone who didn't have somewhere else to go. Catherine's found this is the way Austin works, he's always over the top. He thinks and works in extremes which can be good at times but has also caused issues.

Adjustments also had to be made because of Catherine's physical disabilities. Catherine had a lot of nerve damage from her spinal fracture caused during the attack. She'd only been walking for about a year when they were married. Although she had regained more movement in her legs, they still moved stiffly and she continued to experience a lot of pain. At times it felt as though all of the nerves up her back were igniting in pain, particularly her sciatic nerve. The sciatic nerve is the largest nerve in the body and runs from the top of the hip, down the back of the thigh and calf, to the back of the foot. Catherine describes the pain as feeling like someone stabbed an icepick into her calves, foot, or side. The pain is unpredictable, she never knows which day it's going to be worse. On worse days she has to take everything a lot slower and they had to find balance with this. Austin has had to learn to be extra patient on those days. Another challenge from her nerve damage is her body can't properly adjust it's temperature in certain spots. From hip to knee she's always hot so she often sleeps with a blanket from her knees down and waist up, which can make sleeping comfortably in the same bed difficult. About a year after they were married Catherine reinjured her left knee, further limiting her mobility on that side. When she's sitting down her body struggles to send the message to her foot to be able to lift it. Putting on socks and shoes, walking upstairs, and getting into cars on the passenger side are difficult for her. She's learned about a hundred different adaptations to help her manage these daily tasks. It also affected where they were able to move because it needed to be somewhere without stairs so Catherine could easily move around.

Their first year together was difficult. They were adjusting to a new living situation which ended up becoming more complicated because of Austin's family. They faced a lot of backlash from friends, family, and even strangers because of their marriage. Throughout it all they learned to lean on each other for support. Austin and Catherine agree that throughout their marriage they've had times that comparatively were more difficult and times that were easier. For them it's been an ebb and flow. Whether it's a mental illness or a marriage, there will always be good days and bad days, but it's about choosing to support each other and stick together through it all.

CHAPTER 6

Marriage and Mental Illness

Any married couple will admit that marriage has its challenges. Having a mental illness doesn't necessarily mean there's more challenges, it sometimes just means there are different ones. Austin and Catherine have dealt with issues that had nothing to do with their mental health but there have also been unique challenges related to their mental illnesses. When they got married they both knew about each others' diagnoses and had an understanding of how it might affect their relationship. Not every couple has the opportunity to prepare themselves in this way. A mental illness can surface a lot later in life depending on the environment and experiences of a person. This can present other challenges that Austin and Catherine never had to experience together, like symptoms before treatment, initially receiving treatment, and possibly the start of taking medication. Austin and Catherine faced other challenges common for people who have mental health conditions such as breakthrough symptoms and financial struggles.

Both Catherine and Austin sometimes experience breakthrough symptoms. These are symptoms that happen even though a person is receiving treatment. For Austin this means becoming more argumentative towards authority figures and being paranoid about a lot of situations. He thinks people are out to get him, talking about him, or trying to bug his phone. Sometimes he hears things like his computer talking to him and he watches their door camera more frequently because he's paranoid that someone is sneaking around outside of their home. Austin gets irritated by these symptoms but he accepts it's something that comes with his schizophrenia and medications. Catherine has breakthrough symptoms as well. She experiences flashbacks from her attack and can become hypervigilant and startle easily. Nightmares often disrupt her sleep, causing her more pain which limits her mobility the next day. Austin's medication causes him to sleep heavily, meaning he doesn't usually wake up when Catherine has a nightmare, so he's unable to help her calm down. When Catherine has breakthrough symptoms Austin can become very concerned and protective. Due to his schizophrenia he often automatically thinks of the extreme scenario of a situation. For example, if Catherine is experiencing any kind of pain, he assumes she's dying. She has a difficult time convincing him that it's just from her not sleeping well the night before. It causes Austin a lot of stress because he's constantly concerned and catastrophizing but it's difficult for Catherine as well because she feels she needs to help Austin while she's trying to manage her own symptoms.

Austin's schizophrenia makes him paranoid about situations that other people might not typically worry about. When they were first married Austin was constantly afraid Catherine would leave him. He thought every day would be the day she saw something she didn't like about him and leave, but Catherine was always there the next morning, the one after that, and fifteen years later. Austin still feels insecure sometimes and worries Catherine will leave. The paranoia symptom of his schizophrenia is partly to blame, but it also has to do with how people treat him. When everyone around him acts like Catherine is doing him a favor by being married to him it's difficult for him to believe she'd actually want to stay with him. Catherine tries to be patient and reassure him but, at times she gets frustrated because she has to be so careful of what she says around him. If she talks about going to see her brothers or a music festival in Oklahoma, Austin assumes she's going to leave him and never come back. Even when she's frustrated she doesn't blame Austin though, because she knows it's a part of his schizophrenia and the stigma he faces.

Another symptom Austin experiences is difficulty reading body language. Austin and Catherine agree this is one of the most difficult mental illness related challenges in their marriage. If Catherine is quieter than usual or acts differently in any other way Austin thinks she's mad at him. It upsets Austin because he worries he did something wrong and it's tiring for Catherine because she has to be very conscious of her words and actions. Austin isn't able to pick up on hints from body language or facial expressions and because of this Catherine has to be explicit about what she's feeling so he doesn't make assumptions. A symptom of Catherine's PTSD that presents challenges for the couple is she startles easily. This is amplified by her loss of hearing in one ear. Austin sometimes yells so she can hear him but it makes her jump and have tremors. Catherine jokes that sometimes she ignores him on purpose to get some peace and quiet. All of these symptoms can be frustrating for Catherine and Austin but it forces them to work on their communication skills which have been helpful in their marriage and other areas of their lives.

At times finances have also been a struggle for the Mardons. They're both quite frugal, but they've been on limited incomes for a long time. Finances can be a challenge for people who have a mental illness or a disability because they aren't always able to work full time or at all. A study done in the United States found that people who had moderate or serious mental illnesses were employed less often and at lower salaries than people without a mental illness (Luciano & Meara, 2014). The severity of a mental illness can make it more difficult for someone to work but, unemployment is also likely due to discrimination from employers. Another study found that someone with a history of mental illness was less likely to get a callback for a job than someone without a history of mental illness, even if they had the same resume (Hipes, Lucas, Phelan, & White, 2016, p. 13). Discrimination and stigma towards people who have a mental illness make it more difficult for them to be hired and even if they're hired they may be treated differently, as was seen in the former study where their income was lower. Austin is on AISH, Assured Income for the Severely Handicapped, which is a fixed monthly income he receives from the Government of Alberta. According to the Government of Alberta website (2020), to be eligible for AISH you must have a medical or physical impairment that is likely permanent and severely impacts your ability to earn an income (p. 9). AISH considers the income of both you and your spouse to determine eligibility (Government of Alberta, 2020, p. 9). Austin and Catherine believe this somewhat discourages people with a mental illness from getting married because if your partner makes a certain level of income you'll be taken off of AISH. This places all financial burdens on your partner. The rules of AISH make it very complicated to be married whether one or both partners are on AISH. When Catherine and Austin got married, $200 a month was deducted from his AISH because Catherine was receiving a social security pension from the states. Catherine applied for AISH when she moved to Canada but she doesn't receive very much because of her social security. Since they're on a limited income the Mardons try to recycle a lot of things. They either go to the reuse centre or take unwanted items from friends and thrift shops. It not only saves money and helps the environment but has become a bit of a hobby for them as well. They've found different ways like this to help save money on their limited incomes. Neither of them has ever felt they need a lot of money to be happy but they do need to make enough to cover their bills.

Applying for AISH and other benefits means a lot of paperwork for the couple and this is where most of their arguments stem from. They have personal paperwork for AISH but they also handle a lot of paperwork for their foster sons, getting them on AISH and PDD as well. Then they have the paperwork that comes with running their non-profit organization. They have personal taxes and business taxes and provincial and federal paperwork... it's never ending! They think they're finally done and then they get a call and find out they forgot to file something. They both find the paperwork to be exhausting especially when Catherine is having a day with more pain. On those days Austin tries to remember to be extra patient with Catherine but it can be difficult when he's under the pressure of deadlines. It's been a challenge for them to find a balance with it and not spend every minute doing work.

Mental illness can bring a variety of unique challenges to a relationship. Some of them are directly between the couple, like experiencing and supporting each other through symptoms. Other challenges are more external like finances, paperwork, and stigma. Having a mental illness or disability doesn't mean someone can't have a long lasting relationship. As Catherine said, every relationship has challenges. Sometimes marriage just requires some extra patience and communication. A lot of the struggles the Mardons have faced haven't even had to do with either their mental health or physical disabilities. They've experienced hurdles from meddling family members trying to deport Catherine, foster children being arrested, and neighbours trying to break in. The Mardons joke they don't need a TV because their life is already so full of entertainment. They see their mental illnesses as just another part of themselves and their marriage, there have been challenges because of it but challenges come with every marriage. Their mental illnesses have taught them a lot and made them stronger both as individuals and as a couple.

CHAPTER 7

Supporting Each Other

Although Catherine and Austin have faced a lot of challenges throughout their marriage they've always been each other's biggest supporters. Admittedly, there have been times where they didn't have any other supports so there really wasn't any option but to lean on each other. Throughout their years together they've also learned to advocate for each other when they couldn't for themselves.

Being in a relationship with someone who has a mental illness can at times mean they need more support or different support than someone who doesn't have a mental illness. Austin can sometimes go to extremes when he worries about Catherine because of his paranoia. It can be frustrating for Catherine but it can also be helpful at times because he's very protective of her. He's a strong advocate for her getting the care she needs, whether that's getting an MRI in only four days instead of being on the waitlist for months or talking about treatment with her psychologist and doctor. Catherine supports Austin by calming him down and reassuring him when he has paranoid thoughts. He's not always able to trust his senses because he sees and hears things that aren't there. Catherine acts as a sounding board so he can check if what he's experiencing is a hallucination or reality. Austin and Catherine have somewhat of an advantage in supporting each others' mental health because they both have lived experience with a mental illness. They're able to understand each other because they know what it's like from the inside. They don't have the exact same diagnosis or experiences but they have a closer starting point than someone who has never experienced mental health challenges. That being said, it doesn't mean someone who has a mental illness can't be in a relationship with someone who doesn't! Ultimately it's about being empathetic, patient, and willing to learn how best to support each other and yourself.

Although the Mardons each have their own lived experience with mental health challenges, they also educated themselves on each others' diagnosis. Austin learned about PTSD so he could better understand what Catherine experiences daily. He's learned some of her triggers over the years, but there are so many it can be difficult to notice them all. Austin was diagnosed with PTSD several years ago as well. It was triggered by events that happened when he was in the military reserves in the 1980's but he wasn't diagnosed until recently because his doctors always focused on treating his schizophrenia. His experience with PTSD and treatment helped him understand Catherine even more. Catherine was quite familiar with schizophrenia, having worked as a lawyer for people with various mental illnesses. She's learned a lot more about schizophrenia over the years of being married to Austin, particularly specifics about his medications and their side effects. They sometimes go to each other's doctors appointments so they can support each other in advocating for their needs as well as learn about where they're at with their mental wellness. Catherine and Austin have learned the more they know about each others' illnesses, the more effectively they can support each other. Becoming more educated about someone's diagnosis and symptoms is a step towards learning how to be there for them.

Austin's been on medication to treat his schizophrenia symptoms for more than thirty years. He promised Catherine when they were married that he would take his medication. Catherine has always been a huge supporter of Austin staying on his medication because she knows it helps him manage his symptoms. Austin thinks if he didn't have someone who supported him so fully then it would've been a lot more difficult to continuously take his medication. They saw this firsthand with some of the people who were in their foster boys' lives. Some of the boys had family or significant others who didn't believe in medication or didn't like the side effects of it and encouraged them to stop taking it. This made it a lot harder for those boys. Some of the boys who stopped taking their medication struggled to control their symptoms which led to them acting out in ways they otherwise might not have. The side effects of medication can be another reason that people stop taking it. Side effects can vary depending on the type of medication and the individual. They can be frustrating for both the person taking the medication and their partner. Oftentimes it takes a lot of trial and error to find the right medication that works best and has the least amount of negative side effects. Austin feels the medication he's on now works well for him, but he's tried a lot of different ones over the years, some of which had horrible side effects. Austin's old medication used to make him sleep most of the day. Although Catherine jokes she might actually be able to get things done if that were still the case, it was difficult to endure. Finding the right medication was a frustrating process for Austin because a lot of his psychiatrists and nurses didn't understand what it was like to be on it and the side effects that came with it. Catherine experiences side effects from her own medication as well so they're both able to understand what it's like from personal experience. One major side effect of both of their medications is weight gain. This is a common side effect for a lot of medications but it can be a difficult one for people to deal with. Some people choose to go off of their medication because of it. Austin and Catherine recently joined a weight loss program to help them eat healthier and lose weight. They've been supporting each other with this by working towards their goals together and encouraging one another. They're both happy with the medication they're on now, though they think they'd still be together regardless of whether that were the case.

Sometimes people who have mental health challenges need extra support from the people around them but is there such a thing as too much support? In some relationships, particularly when mental illness or addiction are involved, people can become codependent. This means one or both people in the relationship feel their worth is derived from helping the other person, they focus so much on helping that they ignore their own needs, even to the point of enabling their partner's destructive behaviors (Martin, 2020). The term however is rejected by some psychologists because there's limited scientific evidence and it may negatively stigmatize the basic human need for connection and desire to help loved ones (Psychology Today). Austin and Catherine are among the latter group who don't agree with the term. They see themselves as interdependent or symbiotic because they both rely on each other to bring important qualities to their relationship. There are things that one of them can do that the other can't and vice versa. They watch out for each other and take care of each other but they don't try to be each others' doctor. They're slightly more advanced in their medical knowledge compared to other couples because they have to help each other with things like taking medication but they don't take over treatment of the other person. Catherine and Austin tease each other like any husband and wife would and they don't coddle each other or treat each other like a child. Austin feels their relationship has actually helped them both recover from their mental illnesses.

Both Catherine and Austin have outside supports they can lean on as well. Austin has his doctor and psychiatrist and Catherine has her therapist.

Austin also used to be involved with the schizophrenia society. They're both involved in their church community as well. Catherine's family has been a big emotional support for them, however it's difficult for them to do more because they live so far away. They also have some friends they can lean on and the students they work with are a support as well. Catherine now has friends in cadets she can call if she needs help too. However, when they were going through some of their most difficult times they didn't really have any supports except for each other.

Taking care of each other in a relationship is important but so is taking care of yourself. Through couples counselling Catherine and Austin have learned the importance of self-care and doing activities for themselves. For Catherine, this means playing the baritone horn. She's always been musical and used to play the trombone, guitar, and mandolin. Although she's no longer able to play those instruments because of the injuries to her hand from the attack and her arthritis. When Catherine first started playing the baritone she didn't think she'd be able to. Because of her brain injury she had a difficult time learning anything new. Within five months of playing she noticed something began to change. She was more easily able to do things that she'd struggled with after the attack, like mental math. Catherine actually took an IQ test and they found her IQ had improved significantly. When even other people began to notice she really began practicing more. Playing the baritone is something she really enjoys but it's also helped her build back confidence that she'd lost after her brain injury. It greatly improved her mental health and her cognitive functioning which she wasn't expecting. Austin recently found a passion for vintage board games. Catherine is exasperated by it because he doesn't actually play the games but he really enjoys finding and collecting them. Austin's real passion though is mentoring students through his non-profit agency. He doesn't see it as work because it's something he truly enjoys. Austin thinks he would've made a good professor because he likes to challenge the students to try new things and consider topics that might not have occurred to them before. It makes him happy to see their progress and he feels it's rewarding to be contributing to their futures. Catherine and Austin have learned they need to take care of themselves and practice self-care in order to be able to be good partners to each other.

The COVID-19 pandemic has caused a lot of challenges for everyone and mental health has become a big concern. Austin has developed a lot of anxiety around leaving the house and interacting with people, which is a common fear for a lot of people right now. Catherine has the opposite problem. Throughout the pandemic she hasn't had to deal with a lot of her regular triggers like large crowds because people haven't been allowed to gather in large groups for over a year. Catherine thinks she'll struggle more as restrictions lift and she's around more people. Her and Austin are mentally preparing themselves to deal with more breakthrough symptoms because of this. They plan to continue doing curbside pickup shopping as a way to help lessen Catherine's stress. Like most people, Austin and Catherine have been cooped up with pretty much just each other for company which has inevitably led to more arguing and getting on each others' nerves. They've tried to be supportive of each other by being patient and extra kind towards one another. They've also used a lot of the extra time they've had during the pandemic to work on their mental and physical health and have encouraged each other towards these goals.

Catherine and Austin have been each other's biggest supporters from the beginning. They've learned how to support each other, ask for help from others, and support themselves. Sometimes people may not know how to support a partner with mental illness, which is something Austin and Catherine have definitely experienced as well. They agree sometimes the best support you can give is listening to their experience and validating their feelings.

CHAPTER 8

Foster Kids

Catherine and Austin knew they wanted kids but for various reasons weren't able to have their own. The Mardons had thought about adoption but their first foster child somewhat fell into their lives. This began a chain reaction of fostering upwards of ten other young men. They've been foster parents, adoptive parents, mentors, advocates, and friends to these boys, all of which have some form of a mental illness. There have been moments they've loved and times that have caused them a lot of stress, but they've continued to open their home and hearts to more young people.

Catherine had experience fostering kids when she lived in the states. She'd taken in her nephew for a number of years and then her friend's sons for fifteen years. Austin and Catherine fostered their first boy together in 2012. They'd known Brett since he was a child, having met him and his mom at church. They often helped his mom pick up her foodbank hamper and paid Brett to do odd jobs for them like shoveling snow. When he was a teenager his mom became sick and they promised to look after him if she was admitted to the hospital or passed away. When his mom did pass, the Mardons rented an apartment on the floor above their own and moved Brett in. They applied to be his legal guardians so they could help with his education, medical care, legal matters, and overall well-being. Making it legal allowed them to receive money from the government so they could better provide for him. Brett had been homeschooled by his mom for a number of years, so Catherine and Austin placed him back in school but he struggled and often skipped class. Eventually he quit school to get a job, but he had trouble with that as well. Knowing he had bipolar disorder the Mardons applied for him to begin receiving AISH but they needed a second diagnosis as the first psychologist hadn't properly explained the extent of his mental illness. When they took him to the assessment they were shocked to learn he also had Fetal Alcohol Spectrum Disorder.

FASD is often mistaken for other disorders or goes undiagnosed. Just a few of the symptoms of FASD are challenges with learning, memory, attention, language, motor skills, controlling behavior, reasoning, impulsivity (Government of Canada, 2017). Brett had grown fairly good at hiding some of his symptoms and he didn't show any of the physical traits such as lacking the ridge between his nose and lip or smaller eyes. Although they were surprised, the Mardons still accepted and loved Brett and continued trying to get him the support he needed. Catherine and Austin chose to wait until Brett turned 18 until they officially adopted him. They didn't want to have to worry about causing issues with his family members and they wanted to make it clear it was Brett's choice. Catherine, Austin, and Brett definitely had their challenges together over the years. Brett fell in with some bad groups and eventually moved out of Catherine and Austin's place. Their relationship has improved over the past few years and Brett is doing well. Although he doesn't live with them they see and talk to him often and are proud to call him their son.

Brett was Catherine and Austin's first experience of mentoring and fostering young men but he certainly wasn't their last. When he lived with them he often brought friends to stay in the upstairs apartment and most of them had FASD. Catherine and Austin helped a lot of them get on PDD and AISH and advocated for other support they needed. When Brett moved out, the Mardons put their names on the adoption list and began fostering other boys. All of the boys they've looked after were diagnosed with FASD and about to age out of care, usually around 18-20 years old. Without Austin and Catherine these boys would've aged out of their foster or group homes without being fully prepared to live on their own. In this way, the Mardons see themselves as the last line of train tracks before these boys are dropped in the wilderness. They've become legal guardians for a couple of the boys but don't receive any funding from the government because the boys are all over 18 years of age. They choose not to take full legal responsibility by adopting in order for the boys to still be eligible to benefit from government assistance programs like the public trustee who helps oversee their finances. Catherine and Austin think in a way this helps their relationships with the boys as well because it makes it clear they aren't doing it to get paid. For some of the boys it's their first experience of having someone in their life who is there for them solely because they genuinely care about them. Catherine asked one boy what his favorite candy was to put in his stocking. He said he didn't know because he'd never gotten treats so wasn't able to figure out what he liked. There were a lot of small acts of care like this that other children take for granted that these boys had never experienced until meeting Catherine and Austin.

The Mardons view themselves as more than foster parents, they try to be mentors to these young men as well. The majority of them had turbulent childhoods being moved in and out of group homes. They were never taught skills required for living on their own. One of their foster boys always ran out of food and money before the end of the month. He'd never had to cook, buy groceries, or make a budget for himself. A lot of the boys weren't taught those skills or given the opportunity to learn them, so it was no shock to the Mardons when they weren't able to do them. Austin and Catherine always made sure to leave extra food in the freezer for him until he learned to budget better. Another boy has agoraphobia. The Mardons often bring him pizza both as a treat and to give him some socialization. He enjoys Austin's bad jokes almost as much as the pizza. Austin and Catherine were once asked to a group home to talk about education with one of the boys. It ended up being a four hour discussion about their education and what it's taught them. After the conversation, the boy chose to go back to school. Some of these boys like Brett hadn't witnessed a healthy relationship or marriage. Austin and Catherine were role models for them in that sense as well, teaching them how to treat each other with respect and kindness.

Having a mental illness has allowed Austin and Catherine to relate with the boys in a way that a lot of other people haven't been able to. For example, one of the boys was bothered by developing shaky hands. Austin showed him that it happened to him too and explained it was because they were on the same medication. Knowing someone shares a similar experience like that can decrease feelings of isolation. Some of the boys also have PTSD, which both Austin and Catherine have experience with as well. Although they don't have the exact same experiences as the boys, they're better able to understand what they've gone through. One of the boys said he was blessed to have them as his second family because they understood his PTSD and trauma the way no one else ever had, not even his doctors or social workers. Austin thinks the government is great at the paperwork part, but they're not good at the part that he and Catherine are, which is parenting. For a lot of the boys, Catherine and Austin are the first consistent people they've had in their lives. They're used to changing foster homes and group homes and social workers leaving after a few months. Some of them aren't sure about Catherine and Austin when they first meet, but then it's been a year and they're still around and slowly trust starts to build. When Austin was diagnosed, doctors told him his life was over but he's learned it actually just changed and he needed to make some adaptations. He tells the boys he's had a good life with his diagnosis and helps them believe they can too. Austin and Catherine were written off by a lot of people, just like these boys have been, but they hope to make a difference for them.

Austin and Catherine also act as advocates for the boys they foster and other young people. If politicians are debating a new law or program related to homeless youth or foster care, they can't usually just call them to ask their opinion, so instead they call the Mardons. Although they don't always like what the Mardons suggest. There was one instance where Catherine and Austin were consulted by the health minister regarding the health alert for a syphilis outbreak in the homeless youth population. There was free STD testing, but the issue was you needed to have an ID. A lot of youth experiencing homelessness don't have ID's because they've used them to pay for something, it was stolen, or their parents kept it, and it's hard for them to get another one. The health minister didn't understand this because he'd never experienced homelessness. In his eyes it was easy to get another ID if you lost yours. Austin and Catherine tried to explain the problem with needing an ID to get an STD test. Unfortunately, they didn't listen and further restricted access to health clinics. Upset by this, Catherine and Austin realized they can't change everyone's minds. They continue to be advocates because they believe they're one of the few advocating for the best interests of the youth rather than from a position of power or for monetary gain.

Despite the challenges over the years, Catherine and Austin feel they've learned a lot from their foster boys. One of the most difficult things being how to set boundaries. They began seeing a counsellor when Brett was living with them to help with this. Austin and Catherine realized they have to have a united front. They need to be on the same page and communicate well or it's easier for them to be manipulated against each other. They also learned they have to come first, both as a couple and individually. It's like being on a plane when they tell you to put your oxygen mask on first before helping anyone else. The boys aren't always happy about this but Catherine and Austin know they have to hold their ground or they'll burnout and won't be able to continue. Part of this is ensuring they take time for self-care. Austin enjoys mentoring students and writers through their non-profit organization, the Antarctic Institute of Canada. While Catherine enjoys playing her baritone and helping with cadets.

There's a lot of negativity towards people who have a mental illness having children. Austin was told Catherine should get an abortion if they got pregnant because he was genetically defective. Various studies have shown about one fifth to one quarter of children have a parent with a mental illness (Reupert, Maybery, & Kowalenko, 2013). It's important to note while there are some genetic links to mental illness, environmental factors play a large part as well and there are many protective factors (Reupert, Maybery, & Kowalenko, 2013). In short, having a mental illness does not predispose you to being a poor parent (Reupert, Maybery, & Kowalenko, 2013). Other studies have found that the stigma from having a parent with a mental illness may actually play a large part as well. Children receive associative stigma, meaning they receive stigma for being connected to someone with a mental illness and this may be in part due to people believing they will develop that mental illness (Koschade & Lynd-Stevenson, 2011). This reinforces the idea that sometimes more harm can come from outside factors rather than solely genetics. The Mardons faced a lot of skepticism for fostering the boys. People thought they must have an underhanded reason for being so willing to help them. Austin and Catherine are often asked why they do this. When they met Pope Francis in 2019, he even asked. The Mardons don't have a hidden agenda though, they care for the boys because they want to make a difference in someone else's life. They want them to know they can have a fulfilling life regardless of their past or their mental illness, just like Catherine and Austin have.

CHAPTER 9

Couples Counselling

As grateful as they are to have the boys in their lives, there have been times it's brought them a lot of stress as well. Some of the boys were in pretty volatile homes where they learned some unhealthy behaviors. A few of the boys, particularly Brett, became skilled at manipulating people as a survival skill and sometimes this led Austin and Catherine to be pitted against each other. Brett would tell Austin one thing and Catherine a different thing and they didn't communicate well enough to be on the same page with how to deal with it. They were under so much stress it felt like they were caught in a riptide. Just when they thought they'd reached the surface and could take a breath, they were pulled back under. While fostering Brett they decided to attend therapy.

Their hope was to work on communication skills, setting boundaries, coping skills, and supporting each other. Eventually it expanded from talking about the boys to Catherine and Austin's PTSD as well as Austin's schizophrenia. Communication problems and lack of emotional intimacy are the two most common reasons couples seek both in person and online counselling (Roddy, Rothmna, Cicila, & Doss, 2018). There are a lot of different reasons a couple attends counselling, just like there's a lot of different reasons an individual might. Marriage counselling doesn't always have to be specifically about the relationship, a lot of times it addresses outside stresses like it did for Catherine and Austin. The Mardons initially sought help for parenting skills but this blossomed into working on other topics like supporting each others' mental health. For them, it's become more about addressing their individual needs but both are usually present to be a support. There's a misconception that counselling is only for couples who have cheated on each other or as an alternative to divorce. It's similar to how some people believe individual therapy is only for people who have something 'wrong' with them. The misconceptions and negative stigma can discourage people from seeking therapy when they need it.

Austin wishes they would've tried couples counselling sooner but his psychiatrist had always had a negative opinion of it which deterred him. Some psychiatrists don't think people who have schizophrenia should do talk therapy. If someone with schizophrenia is well, they think talk therapy will complicate recovery because of the emotions it brings up. Austin disagrees and believes talk therapy has been extremely helpful for him. In general, going to therapy has become slightly less stigmatized in recent years. However, couples counselling continues to be surrounded by stigma and misinformation. Resorting to marriage counselling is seen as admitting there's something seriously wrong with a relationship or it's some kind of last ditch effort to save a relationship. Because of the negative stigma associated with it, people tend to worry what others will think of them if they find out. Austin feared people would think they were having marital problems. He doesn't even like going to events without Catherine because he's anxious people will ask him if they've broken up. Catherine on the other hand, wasn't worried about people finding out. At this point she'd already published her book Curveballs which shared a lot more personal details than attending counselling. She figured it was no big deal to have everyone know one more secret about her. In actuality, a lot of people in healthy and happy relationships go to counselling, even former president and first lady Barack and Michelle Obama. Despite Austin worrying what others would think, Catherine and Austin openly told some people about them attending counselling. Certain people like Catherine's mother disapproved of any type of counselling. She'd grown up being self-reliant in a place where people don't like to admit they need help with anything. Telling a stranger your problems was a concept she couldn't wrap her head around. For a long time Catherine had these same feelings but over the years of individual therapy she became more comfortable with the idea and was no longer ashamed of it. Even now, Austin chooses not to tell his mother about couples counselling because he's unsure how she'd react. Catherine feels tragic events like 9/11 and the Felicity bombing in Oklahoma started making it more acceptable to talk about mental health and seeking help. It normalized PTSD as being something people other than war veterans could have.

Another fear Catherine and Austin shared was that counselling wasn't going to help. They'd gone through pre-marital counselling through the catholic church but that was different. It'd been about ensuring they were both ready to commit to marriage, prior to the stress and challenges they'd faced and it was extremely brief. Catherine did have some positive past experiences with therapists but also had some that weren't quite as helpful. The last counsellor she'd seen before leaving Florida was a student. He actually ended up switching specialties after a few sessions with Catherine. She always felt somewhat responsible for scaring him off. Similar to Catherine, Austin had had some traumatic experiences with his counsellors. He'd actually been to couples counselling with his ex-wife at the same place he and Catherine went. During their first session she said she wanted a divorce and Austin was afraid the same thing would happen with Catherine. Austin worried the counsellor would pick sides and blame him for everything. Even though counsellors aren't supposed to pick sides or place blame, it's a common fear for a lot of couples. Skepticism due to past experiences, others' opinions, and fears about what will happen or if it will work, add to the list of reasons couples don't seek counselling.

Another reason Austin and Catherine didn't get help sooner was because it was too expensive. They were living on a fixed income of AISH and social security due to being unable to work. There was no room in their budget for therapy. Counselling can be expensive, especially long term. The going rate for a registered psychologist in Alberta is $200/hour, which a lot of people can't afford unless they have benefits that fully or partially cover it. The Mardons luckily were able to start couples counselling after they received the Order of St. Sylvester from the Pope. This award allowed them to receive discounted therapy through Catholic Social Services. Of course very few people can get discounted therapy this way. Some places do offer counselling on a sliding scale based on monthly income and some non-profit agencies even offer it for free. However, it can be more difficult to find places that will do couples counselling and don't have a long wait list.

Austin and Catherine began with in person counselling and eventually switched to virtual video counselling. They both thought the latter form of therapy was more accessible and enjoyable. They didn't have to drive anywhere or wait in a waiting room. It was convenient to just be able to log on a few minutes before a session. With Catherine's physical disability it was definitely easier. She was able to attend counselling even if she was having more pain that day. Online counselling, also known as telepsychology, has definitely become more popular amidst the COVID-19 pandemic. However, it's possible it'll be a favored option long after the pandemic because it removes a lot of barriers. If people live somewhere isolated, don't have the means to get to a counselor, don't have access to childcare, or are uncomfortable being seen going in person, telepsychology is an excellent alternative to traditional counselling. There was concern that it was less effective or more difficult to form a connection, but various studies have shown telepsychology is as effective as in person psychotherapy for a range of populations and conditions (Abrams, 2020). The Mardons are just one couple that are planning to stick with virtual counselling even after COVID restrictions are lifted.

Austin and Catherine felt counselling made a world of difference for them. They learned skills they could apply to multiple areas of their lives. They experienced EMDR and learned a lot of different calming techniques like centering. Austin had been taught some of these when he was younger, but learning it again with Catherine reinforced it. He feels like he could calm down in almost any situation now. They learned communication skills, how to set boundaries, and the importance of self-care. Knowing these skills they no longer feel like they're caught in a riptide. Although they still have stress in their lives, they're better able to control it, handle it, and take that deep breath. Some of the sessions they did separately but, the majority of the time it was together. They've transitioned now to two sessions a week, one is just for Catherine and they do EMDR for her PTSD. The other session is mostly for Austin but Catherine still joins him because he likes having her there for support. They've both found couples counselling to be a really positive experience overall and would recommend it to everyone. Catherine and Austin believe that just like any other counselling though, it won't work unless you do the work.

CHAPTER 10

Working Together

Neither Catherine nor Austin work full time but running their non-profit keeps them more than busy enough. Austin founded the non-profit agency the Antarctic Institute of Canada (AIC) in 1985. He started AIC to advocate to have the Canadian federal government increase Canadian research in the Antarctic. Antarctic research was his passion and in 1986 he partook in a NASA expedition to Antarctica where they found hundreds of meteorites. After this, he published countless articles on Antarctic research. In each article he named AIC as the institution. About ten years later he began mentoring students. Austin understood the challenges of standing out as a candidate for masters and PhD programs, having gone through it himself. He wanted to share his knowledge and give students the support he never had. He supported students in writing and publishing scholarly research articles and books. This helped them gain experience and increase their chances at being accepted to graduate school. Austin wanted to be able to help students and young researchers on a wider scale so began applying for various grants and funding, turning AIC into the non-profit organization it is today.

When they got married, Catherine began helping with AIC as well. She handles the student's paychecks and makes sure Austin doesn't have a heart attack from the stress of it all. Austin's role is to oversee everything else. He's constantly on the phone about funding, as well as talking to students about their writing and giving them tips on university and applying for graduate school. Though it's something they're both passionate about and love doing, at times, running AIC has been overwhelming for both of the Mardons. They've come to realize they can't do it all themselves. To avoid burnout they've begun to rely more on the students. Austin believes any good leader knows how to properly delegate so they've been trying to put that into practice. It's beneficial for the students too because they're able to gain leadership experience and see whether being in a leadership position is right for them. Austin tries to let people step up to the opportunity and challenge. His dad always told him that in wars the younger colonels and generals, who were in their twenties or thirties, were always the best because they had energy and were more creative. Austin feels the same way about his AIC students. They always bring excitement and new ideas. Still, there are a lot of things the students can't do. Most of the paperwork and payroll has to be completed by Austin or Catherine. They admit there are some structural problems within the agency but they're ever changing, growing, and becoming better.

Working so closely with a spouse like Austin and Catherine do has its advantages and disadvantages. One of the biggest challenges is the sheer size of the organization and the limited logistical support they have. Again, the never ending paperwork causes a lot of friction between them. This especially happens when Catherine is having a slower day due to pain and Austin has deadlines to meet. Catherine jokes the advantage of her helping is Austin doesn't have to hire the ten people it would take to do all of the work she does. Austin admits he could do without some of Catherine's complaining but recognizes she has good reason to because it's a lot of work. They try to put into practice what they learned from counselling: they have to put themselves as a couple and individuals first. Catherine really doesn't mind helping with AIC. She likes to have a say in how things are done and being able to keep an eye on Austin. Austin doesn't understand certain nuances and doesn't always realize when it's an inappropriate time to say something. Austin thinks running AIC has helped him with this. For example, he's come to know not to say anything too political or it could cause issues. Catherine, having been raised in the south where manners are of the utmost importance, has also taught him a few lessons on tact and decorum. Catherine's favorite thing about running AIC together is spending time with Austin. As much as she hates to admit it, she really loves any time they spend together. Austin is grateful for Catherine's help with AIC because he thinks she's incredibly smart and he loves that about her.

Both of their mental illnesses at times have affected their work. Austin can get paranoid about the students. He worries they're spying on him or are working for the Canadian Security Intelligence Service. Sometimes he leaves confusing messages for the students because of this. Austin's very open about his schizophrenia though so the majority of students are quite understanding. One of the symptoms of Catherine's PTSD is phone phobia. She believes it's one of her most debilitating symptoms because it's held her back from doing a lot. She's okay with talking on speaker phone for interviews when Austin is there and she can usually answer the phone if someone calls. The difficulty for her lies in calling people back, calling to make appointments, or talking to anyone she doesn't know well. Catherine worries if something were to happen to Austin she wouldn't be able to continue AIC because of these fears. Although these symptoms have impacted their work, it hasn't stopped them from doing the work they're passionate about and creating a successful non-profit organization.

Austin and Catherine's mental illnesses have also helped in running AIC. Throughout the COVID-19 pandemic they've received multiple grants that have allowed them to have over 300 students writing for them. The pandemic has been debilitating for many people's mental health, including the students writing for AIC. Having experienced mental health challenges themselves, the Mardons take care to put specific emphasis on the importance of mental health when running their agency. They've encouraged students to talk to them if they're struggling, something a lot of employers don't do. By being so open about their own mental health challenges, it normalizes the conversation for students and emphasizes that getting help is okay. AIC has also acted as a community of support throughout the pandemic. Students are encouraged to work in groups, check in with each other, and attend virtual parties at the end of the semester. Many of the books and articles written through AIC have also focused on mental illness. Publishing more scholarly researched pieces on mental health can help dispel the misconception and misinformation that's been mentioned throughout this book. Through AIC Austin and Catherine have helped students achieve their career and academic goals while also working on and learning about mental health.

Catherine and Austin hope to continue AIC for many more years. They've talked to their therapist about setting boundaries to make it feasible because Austin tends to take on more than they can handle. They haven't quite mastered the work-life balance yet but are continuously trying. Mentoring students is still a source of joy for them and they enjoy the time together. AIC proves having a mental illness doesn't have to hold you back from following career passions.

CHAPTER 11
I Still Love You Like Crazy

Austin and Catherine have been married for over fifteen years. They've shared a lot of amazing memories together from a whirlwind wedding, to running a non-profit agency, to fostering and adopting. They've also faced a lot of challenges together, from the threat of deportation, to family attempts to separate them, to discrimination for having mental illnesses. There have been a lot of celebratory times and some trying times that have happened along the way but they always try to stick together as team Mardon.

The divorce rate in Canada is around 38%. With divorce rates being so high, it begs the question, what are long lasting couples like the Mardons doing to keep their marriage strong after so many years. Catherine said the first thing they did was decide from the very beginning that divorce was not an option. The Catholic church has very strict rules on divorce which they both agreed to when they were married. This forced them to always work their problems out rather than giving up. Austin thinks it's also important not to get caught up in the false realities that tv shows and social media portray because that's not real life. He thinks it gives people impossible expectations no relationship could live up to. Catherine agrees with this, there's no perfect person or relationship. She believes you have to expect crap to happen. It's not going to be sunshine all of the time and you need to be willing to support each other through anything. Not everything went according to plan for the Mardons, they faced a lot of roadblocks which meant they had to learn to adapt and grow together. Austin believes having the mindset of considering themselves lucky to be with each other is also important. He still sees Catherine as a real catch and doesn't want to ever lose her so it makes him work hard to make their relationship work. Catherine feels they have to choose to love each other each day, some days it's easier than others, but they pick each other again and again.

Marriage has taught them a lot as individuals as well. For Austin, marriage has helped him develop his emotional side. He used to be like a Vulcan from Star Trek, living by logic and as little emotion as possible, but with Catherine he's been able to let his guard down bit by bit. He's working on noticing his emotions and being more open about them. Austin talks openly about his schizophrenia in public but he doesn't talk much about the symptoms for fear people will think he's a monster or be scared of him. He's able to talk to Catherine about it though and she can reassure him and relax him when he thinks he hears something or becomes paranoid. Being able to talk about something that he struggled with alone for so long has really helped Austin. Catherine was single for most of her life so just being married has just taught her a lot about being with someone. It taught her small things like how to share a bed with someone other than a dog and bigger things like opening up to someone about her symptoms and learning to rely on them. She was used to making every decision by herself but being married to Austin she's able to bounce ideas off of him and it's really stress relieving. Even if she makes the decision she would've made anyways or they don't agree on the decision, it's nice to have someone to talk to about it and work towards goals with.

When he was first diagnosed with schizophrenia Austin didn't think he'd ever get married. Having a happy marriage that's lasted over fifteen years goes against what every doctor told him would be possible. The advice Austin would give to someone who has been newly diagnosed with a mental illness is to not believe the people who tell you it's the end of your life. He admits there'll be changes that have to happen and you'll have to learn what accommodations and support you need but try not to panic. Austin is proof someone who has schizophrenia can live a happy and fulfilled life. Catherine's advice is to accept your diagnosis. Both her and Austin struggled to do so for a long time and it made it a lot harder for them. Catherine believes one of the hardest stigmas people with a mental illness face is self-stigma. People believe no one will accept them and they don't accept themselves, so they deny their illness and try to hide it. Catherine sees it as being similar to having a physical injury. It'd be like breaking your leg and telling your doctor it isn't actually broken, then proceeding to walk around without a cast and continue your regular daily activities. Austin and Catherine are continuing to work towards making mental health as normalized as physical health.

Their mental illnesses impact their marriage but don't control it. Austin and Catherine think being in a relationship and having a mental illness should not be seen as mutually exclusive. Being in a relationship with someone who has a mental illness doesn't require some set of special skills. Similar to any relationship, there will be ups and downs but it's about supporting each other through it. Catherine's advice for being in a relationship with someone who has a mental illness is to separate the person from the illness. When Austin has breakthrough symptoms and she gets mad, she reminds herself to be mad at the symptoms, not Austin. She also stresses the importance of taking things one step at a time because if you look at the whole problem it'll overwhelm you. This is applicable for mental health challenges or any challenge that happens in a marriage. Austin's advice for being in a relationship with someone who has a mental illness is to accept they're going to have limitations but they're still going to contribute and be a partner. It's about meeting them where they're at but also not infantilizing them.

Both Catherine and Austin have felt at times their marriage has been reduced to their diagnoses. People are fascinated by their mental illnesses without caring to know about the other aspects of themselves and their marriage. Although learning to support and navigate each other's mental health has been important to Catherine and Austin's marriage, it's only a small part of their story. They've had many memories and experiences that aren't associated with their mental illnesses and which we've tried to capture throughout this book. Austin's favorite thing about Catherine is her creativity and how interesting of a person she is. He thinks she's incredibly intelligent and is amazed by her mind. Catherine appreciates that Austin puts up with her. She knows she can be difficult to get along with sometimes because of her stubbornness but Austin doesn't hold it against her. Catherine loves how nothing is ever boring with Austin because he's such an interesting man. Catherine and Austin accept each other's diagnoses and know it's part of who they are but they recognize and love all of the qualities each other has.

In interviewing the Mardons it was made clear how much love there is between them. They tease and banter with each other but also remind each other of their accomplishments and strengths. Their love story may never be featured in a film but it's an actual realistic look at what being in a relationship with someone who has a mental illness is like. It's not all that different from being married to someone who doesn't have a diagnosis. Any marriage isn't easy but Catherine jokes that any day she doesn't kill Austin it's another day of thinking he must be 'the one'. People called Austin crazy because of his schizophrenia and people called Catherine even crazier for marrying him. If this is what 'loving like crazy' is, perhaps more people ought to strive for crazy.

References

Chapter 1

American Psychiatric Association. (2020). What is posttraumatic stress disorder [Web page]. Retrieved from https://www.psychiatry.org/patients-families/ptsd/what-is-ptsd

Bhugra, D., Pathare, S., Nardodkar, R., Gosavi, C., Ng, R., Torales, J., & Ventriglio, A. (2016). Legislative provisions related to marriage and divorce of persons with mental health problems: A global review. International Review of Psychiatry, 28(4), 386-392. doi: 10.1080/09540261.2016.1210577

World Health Organization. (2019). Schizophrenia [Web page]. Retrieved from https://www.who.int/news-room/fact-sheets/detail/schizophrenia

Chapter 2

Tubbs, F. (2019). Discussing mental illness with the person you're dating [Blog]. Retrieved from National Alliance on Mental Health website: https://www.nami.org/Blogs/NAMI-Blog/February-2019/Discussing-Mental-Illness-with-the-Person-You-re-Dating

Chapter 3

Centre for Addictions and Mental Health. (2018). People with schizophrenia account for more than 1 in 10 suicide cases [Web page]. Retrieved from https://www.camh.ca/en/camh-news-and-stories/people-with-schizophrenia-account-for-more-than-1-in-10-suicide-cases

Khalifeh et al. (2015). Violent and non-violent crime against adults with severe mental illness. The British Journal of Psychiatry, 206, 275-282. doi: 10.1192/bjp.bp.114.147843

Nordsletten, AE., Larsson, H., Crowley, JJ., Almqvist, C., Lichtenstein, P., & Mataix-Cols, D. (2016). Patterns of nonrandom mating within and across 11 major psychiatric disorders. JAMA Psychiatry, 73(4), 354–361. doi:10.1001/jamapsychiatry.2015.3192

Stuart, H., Patten, SB., Koller, M., Modgill, G., & Liinamaa T. (2014).

Stigma in canada: results from a rapid response survey. Can J Psychiatry, 59(10), S27-S33. doi: 10.1177/070674371405901s07

Chapter 4

Bhugra, D., Pathare, S., Nardodkar, R., Gosavi, C., Ng, R., Torales, J., & Ventriglio, A. (2016). Legislative provisions related to marriage and divorce of persons with mental health problems: a global review. International Review of Psychiatry, 28(4), 386-392. doi:10.1080/09540261.2016.1210577

Chapter 6

Government of Alberta. (2020). Your Guide to AISH [PDF]. Retrieved from https://open.alberta.ca/dataset/928e010e-6b26-46af-a8e2-8c938e5f1b10/resource/b2665396-f63a-45bf-90fb-15fec0b6e5fc/download/css-your-guide-to-aish-2020-05.pdf

Hipes, C., Lucas, J., Phelan, J.C., & White, R.C. (2016). The stigma of mental illness in the labour market. Social Science Research, 56, 16-25. doi:10.1016/j.ssresearch.2015.12.001

Luciano, A. & Meara, E. The employment status of people with mental illness: National survey data from 2009 and 2010. (2014). Psychiatric Services, 65(10), 1201-1209. doi:10.1176/appi.ps.201300335

Chapter 7

Martin, S. (2020). How to conquer codependency [Blog]. Retrieved from Psychology Today website: https://www.psychologytoday.com/ca/blog/conquering-codependency/202010/how-conquer-codependency

Psychology Today. Codependency [Web page]. Retrieved from https://www.psychologytoday.com/ca/basics/codependency

Chapter 8

Government of Canada. (2017). Signs and symptoms of fetal alcohol spectrum disorder (FASD) [Web page]. Retrieved from https://www.canada.ca/en/public-health/services/diseases/fetal-alcohol-spectrum-disorder/symptoms.html

Koschade, JE., & Lynd-Stevenson, RM. (2011). The stigma of having a parent with a mental illness: genetic attributions and associative stigma. Australian Journal of Psychology, 63(2), 93-99. doi: 10.1111/j.1742-9536.2011.00009.x

Reupert, AE., Maybery, DJ., & Kowalenko, NM. (2013). Children whose parents have a mental illness: Prevalence, need, and treatment. Med J Aust, 199(3), S7-S9. doi:10.5694/mja11.11200

Chapter 9

Abrams, Z. (2020). How well is telepsychology working? American Psychological Association, 51(5), 46. Retrieved from https://www.apa.org/monitor/2020/07/cover-telepsychology

Roddy, MK., Rothman, K., Cicila, LN., & Doss, BD. (2018). Why do couples seek relationship help online? Description and comparison to in-person interventions. Journal of Marital and Family Therapy, 45(1). doi: 10.1111/jmft.12329

www.ingramcontent.com/pod-product-compliance
Lightning Source LLC
Chambersburg PA
CBHW030123170426
43198CB00009B/720